Books by Brooks Haxton

The Sun at Night

The Sun at Night

POEMS BY Brooks Haxton

Alfred A. Knopf NEW YORK 1995

THIS IS A BORZOI BOOK
PUBLISHED BY ALFRED A. KNOPF, INC.

ACKNOWLEDGMENTS

Thanks to my family and friends. These poems could not have been written without them. Caroline Beasley-Baker, Susan Kolodny, Harris McCarter, Joe-Anne McLaughlin Carruth, Anthony Robbins, and Kenneth Rosen gave especially generous and skilled attention to work in manuscript.

Thanks also to the editors of the following publications where these poems appeared, some in slightly different versions: *The Atlantic*, "Falls," "Garden," "The Sun at Night," "Dialogue of Soul and Stone," "The Body of My Brother Osiris Is in the Mustard Seed"; *Beloit Poetry Journal*, "One Drop Spilled from Psyche's Lamp"; *Best American Poems 1992*, "Garden"; *Boulevard*, "Wild Geraniums"; *Gettysburg Review*, "One More Thing," "Repertory"; *Gulf Coast*, "On the Inner Planets"; *Hudson Review*, "Limpopo, Orinoco, or Yazoo," "*Memoires Nostalgiques de Cockaigne*," "From the Outside"; *Jacaranda Review*, "The Blown Rose," "On the Essential Goodness of True Art," "Dilemma"; *New England Review*, "1969"; *One Meadway*, "Invisible Genie Construction Company," "Husband after Dark"; *Ontario Review*, "Saturday"; *Paris Review*, "Horologe," "An Interval of Five Tones Being the Dominant"; *Phoebe*, "To Huitzilopochtli on the Renewal of His Sacrifice, 1992"; *Plum Review*, "Erythronium Americanum," "Liriodendron Tulipifera"; *Poetry East*, "Sonnet at Forty," "Further Revelations on the Planet Wokka," "Keepsake"; *Southern Review*, "Giotto's Angel over the Dead Christ Spread His Arms in Flight," "Catalpa, Meaning Head with Wings"; *Southwest Quarterly*, "Shell"; *TriQuarterly Review*, "Again Consider the Wind," "Crow Call," "Scaffold," "Ray," "Century Flower," "Days," "The Black Raincoat," "The Nature of the Beast"; and *Virginia Quarterly Review*, "Her Parents Brought Suit, But Since She Was Incoherent and Profane," "Two Ladies," "The Learned Hevelius When He Mapped the Moon Found Waters There As Kepler and Pythagoras Had Done," "On the Inundated First Site of the Town of Greenville."

Library of Congress Cataloging-in-Publication Data
Haxton, Brooks
    The sun at night: poems/by Brooks Haxton.—1st ed.
        p. cm.
    ISBN 0-679-44179-4
    I. Title.
PS3558.A825S86   1995   95-4138
811'.54—dc20   CIP

Manufactured in the United States of America
First Edition

For HAYDEN CARRUTH

The most beautiful

of the things I leave is sunlight;

then come stars and the moon's face;

then ripe cucumbers, apples, and pears.

PRAXILLA

CONTENTS

Contents

The Sun at Night

LIMPOPO, ORINOCO, OR YAZOO

We built a log raft of straight logs
lashed snug with twisted ropes of bark.
It floated, and since we were friends and boys,
we let the river slip away with it toward sea.

Enormous trees on shore looked godly, and they spoke,
their voices blending with the river
in the noise of insect, bird, and treefrog,
in the one long voice made night and day by rain.

We held each other sometimes to be warm.
We argued, tried kind words, withdrew.
We took a little swim to cheer us up.

The lemurs looked so tender coming down
along lianas out of the canopy, almost
as if they might bestow lost blessedness,
until they snatched the food.

And orchids, delicate and various, grew wild.
And there were the purest, whitest wading birds
with red eyes and blue legs, and bills
for pickaxing into the skulls of snakes . . .
they swallowed them head-first, still writhing
inside, in the gulping snakelike neck.

A gharial cruising under us broke water,
roared, and circled back. The river
opened into the sea. Our mission
must have been complete, although we could not,
even when we knew, say what it was.

HUSBAND AFTER DARK

After the hard looks, looks away, hard words,
and harder silences between my wife and me
I had come out into the garden in the rain
to squat with the roots in the reviving
mud and to search with my utility light,
to break off the zucchini at the stem
before the ripe seed could shut down the vine.
Prickly hairs on the zucchini leaves brushed
at my wrist between the cuff and glove,
making the cool touch of the raindrops more
than a pleasure a relief. It was a good rain
for the eggplants too, and I liked having it
keep the last hatch of mosquitoes off my back.
Under my wife's shadow on the blinds, kneeling
by now, I leaned in scanning another bush
for the thunderhead-dark, purple-shining fruit
while broad soft eggplant leaves laid
damp hands on my balding scalp. The clustered
drops in the leaf-nap coalesced, broke, and,
into my collar down my back and chest trickling
under the length of my left arm, crept down
through the wrist of the glove into my palm.

THE BODY OF MY BROTHER OSIRIS
IS IN THE MUSTARD SEED

Seed from an early Egyptian tomb,
after water damage to the case
in the *Historischesmuseum,*
sprouted in 1955.

That was the year my brother's foot
slipped on spray-wet log.
He was gone
into the whitewater out of sight.

Just downstream
the back of his head
came up
in a narrow chute.

Between terrible rocks
the back of my brother's head
looked wet and small and dark.
I watched it through the roar.

Through tears, afraid
to pray, I told God
he was swimming. Wait.
He would lift his face.

INVISIBLE GENIE CONSTRUCTION COMPANY

Toward sundown at the beach beyond Rye Marsh
my three-year-old and I threw stones.
I chose one flat enough to let fly sidearm
with a crooked and sprung forefinger, snapping
my wrist the way I learned when I was twelve.
It spun with wobbly axis tilted so that the flat face
slapped onto the molten Sound and took flight,
slapped and flew four times, then skittered down
a six-foot-long groove into the shifting underwater.

Isaac paid all this no mind, but rummaged
through the shells and beachglass muttering
the mantra of his own devise, "Invisible
Genie Construction Company," tips of fingers
skipping over the edges of the razor clams,
the busted snailshells, big blue mussels,
after a rock that needed throwing. This
he lobbed with an uncertain pitch, whole body
lunging, doubtful, a half-step, and leaning
into the hesitation of his grip to open.

And the tumbling arc of it, released,
revolved away into the wind and almost
level sunlight, gone with a note plucked
from the psaltery of translucent water.

THE SUN AT NIGHT

The sun at night, under the hill,
under the alligator in his pond,
under the turtle's dangling foot,
between earth and the spiraled threads
of milk that trickle from the eye
of God into the mortal eye and burn,

the sun that shone into the weeds
and under the lids of dead boys
at Antietam Creek and at Khe Sahn
and into the eyes of five kings
hanged by Joshua outside their cave,
the sun God hanged that day for battle—

night then, in the City of Triumph,
victory cars on bridges, lanterns
in mid-air, bright watercraft, glad singing,
smoke and red wine in the mouth, hands
delicate on harp and flute, and in the dark
beyond great ocean waves great winds . . .

the hero looked back into his little house
where tendernesses passed from face to face,
he looked, and under the five grim trees
he turned away, under the stars and planets
set out over the small hill after
a destination, after the sun at night.

THE LEARNED HEVELIUS WHEN HE MAPPED
THE MOON FOUND WATERS THERE AS
KEPLER AND PYTHAGORAS HAD DONE

Whether the full moon floats
out of a culvert, out of a silo,
up from the kudzu
over the red clay cliffs, or drifts
against the drifted Milky Way,

wherever the moon is in the mind's eye
comes a calm, for the sun explodes
and all day in the brain
which it has formed, for which its warmth
is indispensable, explodes,

whereas the moon is luculent
with uselessness, and true,
its Beauty is beside the point,
and as for the unearthly Seat of Love,
as for the Seat of Wisdom and Tomfool . . .

and as regards the chart of the lunar floods:
the Seas of Ingenuity and Nectar
both are small, the Sea of Cold is the longest,
south of that the tiny Lake of Death
spills into the Lake of Dreams.

MEMOIRES NOSTALGIQUES DE COCKAIGNE

Breath on the window froze. Before sleep,
bed warmers. Samovars. Corn whiskey.
Kissing under the goosedown. Then, long dreams
of animals, and journeys, and the returning dead.

*

Winter nights only the library stayed warm.
From inkstrokes flickering after a thousand years
the words in Aramaic, Mandarin, and Maya
fluttered the tongue and took flight into the mind.

*

Then, first thing in fair weather,
there was the hunt. The trout stream.
Fog in the ruined cathedral. Or pure
laziness with coffee and warm bread.

*

And on the shingle after dusk
while eight-foot combers crashed
into the rattle under the stridulous gulls,
whoever wept felt cleansed.

SATURDAY

By sunrise all the birds already in full swing flew, sang,
walked on the lawn, more brilliant, freer than a boy
could even wish. Watching them from his window,
wanting that lightness in his bones, that swiftness,
that high music in his voice, he flapped his arms
and swiveled his quick head, but it was a boy inside.
His mother wanted him to be a big boy now. He left his room.
But in the kitchen, chairs stood brooding around an empty table.
The stock-stillness of a cornflakes box inside the cupboard
worried him, and no one helped when the refrigerator door
sucked open, and the morgue light came on, and cold air
poured down his anklebones onto his unprotected feet. First,
Mama had said: no noise till after coffee. Then: no more
climbing into her bed and whispering to her in her sleep.
And finally: no more Indian-walking through her room at dawn
to lean over her face (the only ever, only only face) and breathe,
and wait, and breathe her breath, and wait, until she woke.
Still, it was as if an undertow that pulled his feet now
stopped them, toes to the crack under his parents' door.
His father's breathing sounded from inside. He saw, eyelevel
in the knob, a dark troll daring him to pass: it was his own
face. And he took it in both hands, and held very still.

WILD GERANIUMS

Sunlight through the new leaves
warmed the humus, and the yellow horns
of trout lilies hung everywhere.
The day the shade closed, they were gone.
Still, in the marsh, the great egret
leaned forward, leaned, and leaned,
and speared the little yellow perch.
The woods were full of wild geraniums,
five overlapping petals in a cup of lavender,
about the size and softness of your palm.

AN INTERVAL OF FIVE TONES BEING
THE DOMINANT

Five is the sum of this world figured by the senses,
and the tally of the planets to the naked eye,
four directions with one person wandering at the pivot.
Five is the head and hands and feet, the five wounds,
and the five loaves for the hunger of five thousand.

Torah has five books with twice five laws
inside an ark of shittimwood, the twice five curtains
of the tent, the scarlet, blue, and purple linen, stitched
with cherubim, the wooden pillars overlaid with gold
with hooks of gold and sockets made of brass.

After Empedocles, four elements made up the world,
tinged, Aristotle thought, with aether, called
in alchemy quintessence, which is five. The Five Wits,
once upon a time, were common sense (or mother wit),
imagination, fancy, estimation, and remembrance.

In the House of Number, one is union. Two division.
Three joins one more to the halves of being.
Four, two twos, divides division; four seeks judgment.
Five holds two and three in consort. In the pentad
mystery trembles under the star of calculation.

Five enumerates the hand. The fist unclinches and flames
wobble from the upheld palm which is the sign of peace.
Five times a day, Muhammad cries out from his balconies.
Farewell and peace. Beside the corn, the passion flower
climbs the fence and wavers over a green bay full of starfish.

CATALPA, MEANING HEAD WITH WINGS

Stars beyond the black whirlpool of the catalpa branches,
stars of February crusted with blue ice,
the stars, machinery of coalescence, engines of release,
samsara, grains cast burning into the godhead,
yahrzeit candles, crucifers with each a candle, wading,
gone far out one summer night into the shallow bay,
the couple on shore witness, same as usual,
the stars, striking an almost philosophic calm,
with any millionth of a second's pinprick fierier
than altogether every habitation ever torched on earth,
yet calm, almost, and everywhere
in all directions hurtling, those most distant streaming
into the not yet, the not even theoretically conceivable—
a man, a woman, standing from their car on either side now,
closed the doors, that sound definitive, then,
desultory shifting of their boots in ice and gravel, quiet,
they looked up into the bare three-story whorl of the catalpa tree.

GARDEN

I poked my finger in the dirt and put the seed,
and Satan clapped me on one shoulderblade and said,
Most righteous! though of course no one was there.
A crow flew out of the buttock of a thunderhead.
No rain for weeks. I carried water by the doublebucket
under the dereliction of great fleets of cloud.
My shankbones swashed through species of brown grass.
Which time, the seed grew, flowered, and bore fruit,
a fact so biblical I walked between the rows of corn,
green walls to either side, strode forth like Moses
after the exit sign began to flash. And Satan came
again by twilight in the body of a coon, and said,
Ah! hissing from his throat, upreared on hind legs,
black lips curled back from the pointed teeth, and smiling
vanished into the touch-me-nots—the flowers, even
while the light failed, orange as minute live coals.

AFTER THE FALL

He walked back to the road
searching for the wound
with his left hand,
but no lump, no blood,
no torn peel of scalp.
His feet meanwhile found
level patches in the path
among the rocks.
And he could see.
It was a clarity
unlike his usual attention:
minus the focal point.
Light came bounding off the world
into his brain from everywhere,
as if a voice had said, "Behold!"
And he had understood,
and could quit looking, and obey.

FOR HUITZILOPOCHTLI, ON THE RENEWAL OF HIS SACRIFICE, 1991 AD

The lightning in the god's left hand is blue and white.
Feathers green as malachite and blue as lapis and blood red
stand in his crown. His body is a feathered jewel. Hummingbird,
the priesthood call him, Storm God, God of War, for whom
in hecatombs the children quick in the gibberish of their tribes,
the old men, and the women die. For Hummingbird, we thrust up
altars into the air. For him, we fly, proof of the cleanliness
of his conception, him, whose mother's prayer was blameless,
that the crown of feathers fell from heaven onto her naked breast.
For Hummingbird, whose flesh is bread, whose feast is eaten
on the longest night, for Hummingbird in whom we see
the handsome cheekbones of our tribe, we take these enemies,
one thousand, uproot plunging in the air these hearts
for Hummingbird, whose limbs are bluer than blue sky.
As Hummingbird lets go the lightning from his open hand, so!
by the tens of thousands, we release them into the smoke.

ON THE INNER PLANETS

Tu non se in terra, si come tu credi

1 *Following Sundown on Mercury*

I walk at the speed of nightfall west,
about one mile per hour as the crow flies,
  if only the crow could fly, with no air.
    I wish I had a crow. I hate crows,
    but I wish I had one now for company.

Craters, warm rocks, starlight at my back,
  if I stopped walking into the heat
I would be solid ice, until the next day
when the sun scorched off my clothes, and thawed,
    and cooked my flesh black into the bone.

Just now, my mouth is forming words,
but no air carries the waves of sound.
    I could have gone to Teotihuacan,
  and I chose Mercury. There must be reasons,
    maybe the winged hat, maybe the footgear.

Somebody mentioned he was the God of Healing.
As it turns out, there's no god, and here I am.
    "But what it is," a Memphis blues man
    in the jailhouse sang one time,
      "it just don't feel like home."

2   *Venus, in the Mercurial Evening Sky, and Later*

Under a tall rock flared with sunlight at the tip, I stopped.
Night fell. More slowly than the eye could see her move,

the White One rose into a black depth scattershot with stars.
My prayer when I saw her was to die, to be in death with her.

Wherever I was, a woman stood from her bath, looking me
in the eye, touching herself, teasing . . . I felt cold.

And when the trance had passed I lay in total darkness
stretched out on a bed of burning dust. Far off

there were children howling, high shrieks of a woman
tortured, moans of old men, sobs, and pleading screams.

Laughter wracked the molecules of the air. An almost liquid gas
poured into my lungs. Sulfur clung inside my nose and throat.

Eyes useless, fingers drifting over the pitted rocks,
I searched for the others, as if underwater and in flames.

Scoria whirled in the superheated gas. My skin to the finger
felt intact, but hurt the way flesh under a peeled-back blister

hurts even to touch the air. I should be dead, I thought.
Screams blasting through my windpipe scorched my tongue,

and my voice came, like the others, from far away.
It was a human voice, but it was the wind.

3   *Somewhere Nondescript on Mars*

This rustheap of iron silicate and rime is not the same
    as any rock on any other planet besides Mars.
The flakes of galaxies in Berenice's Hair also
        are singular and will collapse
            into the veil of discontinuum.
      To make, therefore, a hymn of praise

    and thanks, or prayer for mercy,
        even to cry with rage, felt noble
when I was alive. I found virtue
        in the ecstasies of the soul.
    Lately, I am not amused at the display
      of what I used to call *humanity*.

    I said that word on Earth
    with such high feeling tears formed.
        I felt little catches in my throat.
I cannot ascertain how genuine this was.
      On Mars I grow more dubious. Still,
    twinges in my pharynx cloud my thoughts.

CODA: *Full Earth near Midheaven*

The nauseatingly small sun went down.

As a boy who kept snakes I was shy like them.
Coral snakes, the deadliest,
were delicate, and difficult to keep alive.
Hognoses were most harmless.
Trapped, a hognose played dead, belly-up.
Turned over, he flipped back into the belly-up position,
body language as exact as speech:
"No. I am dead. I can prove it. Look!"

Before they played dead they would threaten,
but they never bit, so I was not afraid
to see them puff their necks wide like a cobra's.
Still, although I knew
they were non-poisonous, and when they struck
they barely bumped me with their turned-up snouts,
I could not, often as I tried, relax
and watch one strike my hand without, quick, flinching.

So, with the Martian moons at midnight,
when hunched Phobos rolled past Deimos overhead,
I was afraid, but not afraid of
anything. The fear was beyond my power to conceive it.
I do know that a moon should not look dingy or ill-shaped.
And one of these was too small too, and slow.
The other one was worse, too fast,
crazed by the pull, about to fly apart.

I came back as far as Earth's moon.
First thing here, I did the walking tour
of human litter, flags, wrecked hardware, trashheaps.
On the far side, I could remember
when there was consolation
in the unknown and the forbidden.

Now, at last, I'm feeling settled
in the Crater of Copernicus, above the Known Sea,
where Apollos 12 and 14 landed.

Earth looks huge from here, and blue
with ocean, green with leaves and grasses,
desert, cloudswirl, bands of dark rock, threads of white
along the ridgetops over the treeline.
Although green is life,
I stare into the blue more often.
Years pass.

After the heat and cold, sulfuric acid, dust storms,
odd collisions in midspace with asteroids,
what's left of me is bruised and burned
with shreds of muscle dangling, brainslops,
viscera, and fluids leaking
from their chambers, all of which
I feel with pain
as though pain mattered.

Once, in a pensioned room over a bridge, we made love.
While we dressed, we argued. At an impasse,
we walked out together, rain in the ancient street,
and then, hair wet, I stood beside her among strangers
where the layered blue suspended brook trout
all around the feet of Jesus baptized in the wilderness
by Ghirlandaio or someone,
one of the less well known Italian masters.

THE BLACK RAINCOAT

I don't know: I wanted to bring the raincoat maybe
for the weather, if it changed. You got me. It was odd—
the way I laid it out and smoothed and buttoned it.
I folded the arms down, forward, in a V.
This was my wife's coat, OK?
One of those black shiny plastic jobs.
I stepped back from the bed and stared at it.
I mean, I didn't really think I'd wear it if it rained.
It's like I said. I don't know what I thought.
I rolled it up tight like a sleeping bag
and kept it on the seat beside me in the car.
Here we go. I drive straight there,
over the Spuyten Duyvel to the Cloisters parking lot.
I walk right up to the ledge.
I've got the raincoat in both hands.
So there I am. I'm standing there.
I'm worried what comes next.
This was my first time, OK? I felt sick.
My hands were sweating, trembling, I felt dizzy in my stomach—
it was like—you're in an elevator and the cable snaps,
and there I am pretending to admire the view.
I know. It's in the guidebooks. It's a four-star view.
This must be the first weekend in May,
when you can still make out the bridge from up there,
through the leaves. You see yachts on the river.
You can see the Palisades. Maybe
that's your kind of thing, a view. Me,
it made me feel like I would disappear. OK:
I have to let myself unroll the raincoat

on the top of this low wall.
I pick up one arm by the cuff and let it
dangle off the far edge—forty feet straight down.
I take my handkerchief, I stuff it in her breast,
you know, the pocket, neat, like, with three corners out.
Which clicked, and now I could undo the buttons. So:
so far so good. I know there must be people watching me.
I don't need to look around. I know.
There're always people in that park. Young couples. All the time.
I'm thinking how I'll get my wife some red shoes
with stiletto heels, and she can wear this coat, and them,
and nothing else, or maybe one of those black panty girdles
with the lace, the kind that's open in the crotch.
I'm thinking we can turn the lights on bright tonight—
I'll change the bulbs—
and she can stand there, backed up to the window,
with the curtains wide, and I'll be sitting on the couch,
where she can talk to me, and open up the coat, and tell me things.
I'll ask her . . . I can ask her anything. I could too. Hell, I did.
We did all that. It was amazing. Really. She was great.
She thought I might be joking that first night.
It was a joking kind of thing. But right away
she got the feel for it. And I was proud of her,
you know, back then. It's funny, though:
that afternoon, already, I could tell:
it was the coat. It wasn't her.
I mean, I wasn't using *it* to make things good with *her*.
And I'm not saying I used her to make things good with it.
I couldn't let myself do that. But that first time,
while I was getting those first thoughts, about . . .
how we could do it later, after I got home,
I knew the part at home wasn't the part I needed.

The Black Raincoat

I was leaning way out over the wall,
holding the coat up by the shoulders. And I didn't feel sick now.
I was about to let it go.

SONNET AT FORTY

When who I am lost touch with who I was,
I stood into the mirror, flushed the john,
and killed the bathroom light. Outside, the lawn
grew softly in the dark, and not peachfuzz,
but in my palm gray stubble sharp as burrs.
With luck, maybe, just half my time was gone.
I set the clock, unplugged the bedroom phone,
and flexed my toes three times inside my shoes.
But in my skull was what was going numb.
Things weren't that bad, but I had made it all
look that bad with my inept flimflam.
Lying in bed feeling the downward pull,
I could not want back what had felt worthwhile,
or think why who I was picked who I am.

ON THE ESSENTIAL GOODNESS OF TRUE ART

A tick at the tip of a grassblade waved its legs
like any sentimentalist in love,
and gravid hornets mumbled underground.

During the mid-Trecento, besides painters,
oriental rat fleas also thrived,
and buboes, on the beauty of the flesh.

Plague Art *was* nature art. And if,
as my friend the poet said somebody said,
if finding fault with nature is to praise

an essence in the mind of God, praise be
for the enormous mantid in Brazil
which plucked the intestine out of a screaming shrew.

CROW CALL

When a child who eavesdrops on the crows
for secret knowledge finds a black wingfeather
tricked with nits and lice and dabbles it
in holy water, he may keep or lose it, but the stone
that marks his body will be turned to flame.
His grave will be upharrowed and left open.

The crow, meanwhile (under the black sheen of his vestment,
under the cobweb nerves, the whitish pignut skull
with its bad-tasting fruit and beakbones blacked
with rhamphotheca, hidden sex, and heart like ours
with four chambers), whole crow, purpled by broad sunlight,
flies into the heat spell, through sub-zero winter
rules the farmstead, dump, dead milltown. Any bone
or branch latched into the black foot is his outpost.
Every sunrise rears him to cry havoc.

When a forthright child, therefore, has learned the habit
of the crows, taking no thought to understand them,
that child cries their very word among them laughing
after his grave has been forgotten.

1969

Between dances, under the strobe and smoke,
Flora talked with a boy who liked the Dead.
His lip bristled with legs of trapdoor spiders.
Shreds of his voice kept catching in his teeth.
She slipped away into the dorm upstairs,
which was a crypt where she tried doors at random.

*   *   *

Phil woke to the snap of a doorlatch. Hinges mewed.
In ripped jeans and a T-shirt, Flora stood
at the foot of his mattress humming to herself
and sobbing while she ate big purple grapes.
Phil knew her. They had spoken over breakfast once.
Wrapped in his bedsheet, he felt naked. "You're OK?"

"I'm tripping," she said, meaning yes and no.
She pulled her T-shirt off, and when she stretched
her arm-muscles looked big as his.
                                   He stared,
and neither of them spoke, while she stepped
naked out of her jeans and crossed her arms
as if to shield her breasts.
                             "You're watching me,"
she whispered.
               "Yeah. You woke me up. Are you
sure you're OK?"
                 She kneeled onto the mattress.
"I'm wiped out," she said, sprawled on her belly
on top of the single sheet, and fell asleep.

* * *

That time at breakfast she had worn the same
ripped jeans with no bra under her tie-dyed shirt.
He'd asked her how she liked the college. "Fine.
I thought I might do seminary, but . . .
that's not my kind of thing: I'm an Episcopalian."

"I'm nothing. I don't even know for sure
if I'm agnostic." When she laughed, he said,
"Episcopalians are agnostic, right?"

* * *

In Flora's dream she took an orchard path
down into an arbor overhung with grapes
and stepped out onto the riverbank at dusk.
A paddlewheel boat tiered with balconies
came laboring upstream. Ladies in white
waved to her from the rails. They were her sisters,
cousins, aunts, and great aunts in their youth,
their voices delicate with forced hilarity,
their cries of greeting more like calls for help.
A player piano in the boat played rags
with a precision that made Flora wince.
The paddlewheel churned froth. Ichthyosaurs
writhed underwater through ruined temples. Everyone
knew: this was the time of sacrifice.
Their goodbyes were a warning, "Take care! Take care!"

* * *

Curled on one side facing him, she slept
while dawn flurried the dark elm into the light.

Phil accepted the doctrine of Free Love,
but he did not love Flora, or feel free
to touch her, although he did like her breasts,
the small flush sepia-tinged aureoles,
the nipples, the corollas of black hairs,
seven or so on each. Her breadth of cheekbone
and her bent nose gave her a gypsy look.
The dried sweat mixed with sour breathing moved him . . .
and the power knit into the long-boned arms
and legs, how that might flow and fold and overflow
in lovemaking. But something failed to click.

When she began to whimper in her sleep,
he felt ashamed to have been watching her,
as if his thoughts had given her bad dreams.
Laying his left palm on her shoulder, he said,
"It's OK. You're dreaming now. It's all right."
And out of the anonymity of sleep,
she surfaced into a questioning look.

"Weird dream." She pulled the single sheet off Phil
and covering herself glanced down. His mood
looked to be changing. She smiled sleepily,
"I keep waking you up."
                              "No. That's OK."

*　　*　　*

A mockingbird kept singing in the elm,
"Pretty, pretty, pretty . . ." It was dawn.
"Whirrup! Whirree! . . . Kai-cueue, kai-cueue, kai-cueue!"

Flora eased down toward Phil's hips with him
inside. She arched back onto her stiffened arms.

"This feels strange," he said. "Does it to you?"
She let a pent-up breath go from her chest.
There was a catch and flutter. She was in tears.
With a little shrug, she eased away
on the apologetic small sob of her laugh.

FALLS

A poplar cut loose from the bluff upstream floats
into the waterfall in full leaf, branches first,
the breached crown quaking at the lip, then roots
tipped into thin air, all swooped under by the pull
and pelted into the long drop, soaring free.

The eye waits, letting the waterfall rise,
upside down, torched on the retina's raw cup,
back through optic cable into the hindmost lobe
where maps of daylight sputter and go out
past webs and mesh into a flickering thought.

The tree stands on its tipmost leafy branches,
rooted for a second in the vertical white water.
And the eye waits without blinking. Tears form.
Look! The onlooker is moved, the way the tree is,
seeing that the tree is still alive and falling.

FELIS CONCOLOR

Under enormous cottonwoods, in canebrake,
lost, among the cypress knees, the white men
saw big cats, in their tongue *tigre*, puma
to the High Lords of the Inca, whom
Pizarro found it worth his while to kill,
as in good time his countrymen did him.
His officer De Soto died that next spring
here in a swamp beside the Mississippi,
claiming it for God and Charles the Fifth.
It was a fever, said his men. We say so
too. But cougar is the name I like,
from Tupi for false deer. A man thought
venison and saw it through the bamboo leaves.

ERYTHRONIUM AMERICANUM

Trout lily, he said; she said, adder's tongue . . .   ROBERT HASS
In my part of the country it's a dogtooth violet.   HAYDEN CARRUTH

What-was-to-be kept coming back with leaves
to the willow, with late sleet, with a familiar smell
of bark, with mud between the frost and the old ice.

Downed-over scales of pussy willow bud now broke,
first into tatters, then full catkins of white silk,
and all, all that much sooner for it, fell apart.

The trout lily now bloomed, brown trumpet
peeled back into a yellow star, scored
twelve times round inside the bell with rust.

The stem, like a mute swan's upheld neck, tilted
the head in a pose that was almost meek, pike thrust
into the cleft and green and splotched-with-purple tongue.

FROM THE OUTSIDE

Brown leaves made of the hill
a raw sienna cloud. Already
I stood ankle-deep. A leaf
glanced off one shoulder, brown
with a remnant green, and red.

And stooping for it, stumbling,
plunging the heels of both hands
up to the wrist in leaves,

I felt almost, beyond the shock
of solid ground, as though
my body might float through,
as after all it does.

ONE DROP SPILLED FROM PSYCHE'S LAMP

Your throat
by dawnish windowlight,
the purple bloodwell
throbbing in your sleep

toward hidden thought,
these eighteen years
since dawn first showed me
in your sleep

how beautiful you are,
again I see, and turn away,
these few years being
my young manhood, gone.

I hate and love,
a young man cried,
great Latin guttering
in his blood,

and if you ask me how,
he said, or why,
what I can tell you is
I feel it burn.

FROM THE ATTIC OF
THE INSANE ASYLUM GATEHOUSE

I caught a glimpse at dawn of someone (I thought
inmate) walking under my window between banks of snow.
There was a stiffness in his walk, like what you get
on Thorazine. He wore a dark suit with no overcoat.
Along the road wild geese pushed their bills
into the snow to graze. They didn't notice him.
A mist made everything look warm and quiet,
but the drainage pond beside the old incinerator house
was frozen, where the Jews come for atonement,
to throw bread into the moving waters. After a while,
the switchboard operator rang me: there's a guest.
He's waiting for me in the lobby. Yes, (she called me
dear) she did try telling him the way, but he was deaf,
or spoke some other language . . . Greek, who knows?
He had a scrap of cardboard with my name in crayon
scrawled, she said, by must-a-been a kid, a mental case.
I didn't tell her where I thought he came from,
much less whose handwriting it was. I thanked her.
He and I climbed into the stationwagon, him dead quiet.
I was quiet too, but he didn't breathe. At home I parked.
I said, "You must have tried the door. I work
upstairs. The doorbell doesn't reach those rooms."
We stepped out into the snow and mist, and stood there
looking at the trees, big spruces in the yard, white pines,
cedar branches stooped with snow. I thought, why not?
I fetched a bag of stale bread, took him to the pond,
and showed him how to throw crumbs onto the ice.
He didn't care. He fed his to the geese and walked off,

which left me to work out the atonement. I tried again
with running water at the spillway, but no luck. I tried
the scrap of cardboard from my pocket, dropped it in.
Drips melted from the willows into the ditchwater, hitting
the cardboard as it spun away. I must have scrawled
my name like that, in red crayon, a long long time ago.

REPERTORY

The Charles froze all the way across.
I walked out, gazing into the ice
between looks at a tattered xerox:
Freilich ist es seltsam
die Erde nicht mehr zu bewohnen . . .
I must have memorized and half-forgotten that
ten times, imagining Schloss Duino,
Rilke at a stormy height, and in the wind
over the gulfs of the Adriatic
that inhuman voice:
Of course it is odd
no longer to inhabit the earth . . .

After the Rilke, I tried Valéry:
Ô récompense après une pensée
Qu'un long regard sur le calme des dieux!
"The Cemetery by the Sea," which I forgot,
except the opening, about the poet
in the noon sun on his cliff, magnificent,
and somewhere in the middle where a maggot
slips like a teardrop out of a corpse's eye.

But I have never yet burst forth
into the noon fire or the storm
to look from the cliff's edge over the sea.
One cloudy afternoon I did stroll on the cliffs
where Edgar after the storm in *Lear* told
blinded Gloucester he could jump. A seal
swam playfully among the rocks. I felt (like Bishop
on her little precipice beyond the fishhouses) amused
in pleasant company, though doomed, of course,

and plucked loose from the essential element,
the seal's and God's and mine.

After the fish and chips that night
my friend and I drank red ale.
We held hands walking home. Our bedroom
was the back of an old delivery van.
Local boys made catcalls
when they saw it at the roadside wobbling.
Somebody laughed—I thought, almost
despite himself, with tenderness—
and the next day we were gone.

THE NATURE OF THE BEAST

Blunt skull of a jaguar, eye
reptilian, pupil tiny, radiating
gold spikes hatched with blue
and flecked with pigeon blood,
scales iridescent, clouded with dried salt,
between scales tufts of hair—maybe
the larva crept into the rotten eaves,
into the attic where it lived on mice
which we had thought were eaten by the cat
that ran away, only she did not run away.
And now the creature wallowed in our bed.
It breathed a tinge of milk and blood,
while we stood at the doorway looking in.
The lips curved in a smile, thin, wine red,
leathery, and thoughtful in a way sublime
though not remotely human. Black wings
buckled with vermilion flexed and stretched out
over the scaly back. Afraid to run, we looked hard
into the creature's eyes, its eyes, not each other's.

BAR STORY

How'd I know this kid was anybody's wife?
All I know's the eye she give me. It was a rover,
one of these. So I says, "What's your pleasure?"
But this big guy, must be forty, come up
out of the john all in a huff. Steps up.
Here's where things took a turn. She just goes, "Oops,"
and puts her fingers to her lips, you know,
where I can see the ring, but with her eye
on him, like, Yall think yall can handle this?

You been in bars like what this was. It was
big ferns in crocks, fat salesmen in old plaids—
the local girls got party dresses on.
I had me my stitched cowboy shirt. I'm there
trying this credit card . . . which was a gift,
but that's another story. Main thing is,
it's not the kind of place you look for trouble.

So: she come back at me like he's still gone,
"Frank here and me, we're on our honeymoon.
We're celebrating. What's your name?"

                                        "I'm tired."
Frank says, half sideways, looking more at me.

Something about Frank tickled me. I said,
"Frank, please. Let me buy yall some champagne."
And I just grinned, because it's something here
I had to watch. "Post. Daryl Post's the name."
That was the name I went by, on the card.

"Daryl!" she says. "And I'm Cheryl. That's weird.
Don't you think so? Him Daryl and me Cheryl?"

"Mr. Post, you will excuse us," Frank says,
like he owned the steps to heaven can't nobody
climb but college boys. Thing is: Cheryl's bound
to been a barroom tart since she was twelve.

I know this girl. I know: she married wrong,
she knows it, she knows I know, and old Frank
must just be finding out. That's where we are
now while I'm buying us champagne. I made
the toast: "To wedlock, and the padlock. Here's
to locks." So Cheryl giggles and drinks up.

But Frank just looks off, sadlike, and don't drink.
I thought that toast might tickle Frank, a man
with education. I said, "Frank. Here's locks.
Here's keys that go round easy in the tumblers."

This time Frank looked down into his glass,
and Cheryl didn't laugh. It's like the two of 'em
caught wind of a bad fart. So I said, "Frank,
have I got spinach in my teeth? Am I . . ."

All of a sudden Frank says to the bartender
to call the police! Which he does! Look at this:
I dressed up nice and come there like I did
because I figured it won't be no police,
and now Frank's took it on himself to call.
And give my name. When I ain't done one thing
but bought champagne and made some conversation.

Bar Story

Well: I took this here. I used to go out
with an ER nurse and meeting her at work
one time I picked this up. It's whatchacall . . .
a surgical knife. I carry it. Now, what
I done with Frank, I took this out, I yanked
his shirtwaist to his chin, and I just
opened him, up the front. That's all I did.
I just opened him up the front, that's all.

DIALOGUE OF SOUL AND STONE

I was talking to a rock
and I said, "Stone,"
I talk to them like that, I said,
"what makes people feel extraneous?"

To which the rock in its own idiom
replied, "Extraneous's ass!
You think you got it bad.
Try igneous extrusion.
Try a little freeze and thaw.
Try glaciation.
Stand out in the weather for ten thousand years.
We'll talk extraneous."

One thing about rocks:
they cut you half an inch of slack
but never. That's why guys like me
idealize them. I said, "Sage"—
I laid it on a little thick,
this rock I'm talking to,
it's not much bigger than a Chiclet,
but I don't want to give offense,
so I said, "Sage, what
should the human species do?"

To which the rock said nothing,
but he got that look. You know:
they're thinking to themselves,
"Drop dead."

AUBADE OF THE BLOWN ROSE

The rose, the oak, the owl, and I,
The waves palavering with the rocks,
Starlight burst on a blue sky,
And dust grains in the gears of clocks—

I kissed her slowly on each breast
And laid her palm on my cheekbone
And looked out how the foam at the crest
Of a green wave tripped, torn off and blown,

And the blown rose wagged beside the gate
And the owl in the tumult of the oak
Hid in the broad leaves from daylight
As a man's thought hid in what he spoke.

So she smiled, and she said Yes she knew,
And she had agreed, and said goodbye,
When I watched from the gate how the owl flew
And the rose shook, and the oak and I.

SCAFFOLD

Close as I ever come, it had to been
forty feet over a concrete floor, this
speed freak handed me a length of six-inch pipe
weighed near as much as he did. He's wired up,
and I was out of it, into my sad wishful groove,
forgiving everybody, holding hands and all that
in my head. You can't be up that high
and living in your head. But I called home
that night before, a little drunk, collect,
and told Jude how I missed her. She said,
"Yeah," and wouldn't let me talk to the girls.
We weren't separated yet. It was this new job,
had to have one guy with a carpenter's card;
no carpentry, turns out, but they can't fire me.
We were traveling, small towns, nowhere
you could hang out until nighttime; so I worked:
I showed up anyway, with Irish coffee, and did
something, not much, just to entertain myself.
So, this speed freak, he's gone three days
maybe with no sleep, he hands me the pipe.
He sees me going over the edge with it.
And he's too fucking spaced to let me go.
The two of us, we built that scaffold quick—
we only had a couple minutes' work up there,
so now, it's doing this wobbly goddamn dance,
and both of us lean way back off the platform,
catty-corner, holding the pipe between us.
He must be . . . one-forty. I'm two-twenty, plus,
and drunk. I looked him in the face: kind of guy,

Scaffold

he tensed up working; he was a drinker too,
he did that same thing drinking, bore down,
all the time; not now though, now he's giving me
a whole new look. I heaved the pipe so it fell
back onto the scaffold, and it took us with it.
But what gets me—even before I knew
which way we'd fall—what gets me is
the calm I see coming over this guy's face.

DAYS

The days of rain collapsing into the dusk
went day by day by day, and night was day.
Past midnight, sleet dinged into the sleeve
of a window unit—*ding!*—and Mom was awake.

Big pellets clocked into the headboard wall,
ticking the windowpanes. Time, sprung loose
from the blinking digitals, whirled everywhere.
The cracked-off limbs lay flailing in the street.
Wind swung from a traffic light.

        And Mom left Dad face down,
to check the children, breathing, in their sleep,
while something soft as a thrush at a windowpane
kept flinging itself into the side of the house.

HOROLOGE

a tout ce qui fuit   CHARLES BAUDELAIRE

The clock inside the mantid egg under the drifted snow,
    the sap clock in the February tree,
        von Karajan's internal metronome
    with different signatures exact in either hand,
        terns, orcas, caribou in shrunken herds,

        state ministers who synch their talks
into the general's scheme, stock brokers
    taking note, and families at the border with no plan,
        the unhoused axle of the planet wobbling
one half turn among the stars in thirteen thousand years,

        hatched leatherbacks not making for the heavens
        into the surf but pulling onto the highway
with front flippers bloody toward new lights in town, clock
stopped on the mantle, pockmarks of storm systems on the sun,
        ticking from inside a flame-rapt log

HER PARENTS BROUGHT SUIT, BUT SINCE SHE WAS INCOHERENT AND PROFANE

the judge believed the shrink, and on
        her husband's signature she lay
under the tower clock in her restraints,
        a needle in her vein, tube
butterflied onto her arm. The hill outside
        was ice. The anesthesiologist
said, "Now." He squeezed the works and she
        was under: paralyzed: no breath.
Her husband looked down at the pond
        behind the old incinerator house.
Warm spill stumbled into a thawed spot
        from the ditchbed. Helpless,
he had watched her drinking through September,
        picking up odd men,
painting the residue of nightmares, then
        not sleeping, then reporting
that the phone company had put transmitters
        and receivers under her scalp
which finally she had to shave in patches
        to slice open to remove the bugs.

First, she had to leave him: his whole brain
        had been replaced at work
with boards of microcircuitry, no point
        in struggling any more with him,
though she did telephone their children,
        asking if the school nurse
might have scheduled them for odd procedures.
        She called every day.

That first afternoon she missed, he knew.
    He drove straight to the studio
he rented her over the fishmarket. She liked
    the smell. It baffled
ultrasound, she said, and maybe infrared
    and microwaves. It made him
weep. He rang, knocked, slipped
    a plastic card into the latch,
and found her out cold on the bathroom floor,
    hair wet with blood,
phone off the hook, hi-fi and radio and
    television on full blast.

Uphill from the pond, below the hospital,
    a cloud poured from an open pipe
and sheathes of ice formed on bare
    honeysuckles and spirea planted
to conceal the ditch. Elsewhere
    there was a dust of dingy snow.
His fingertips felt cold inside the rabbit
    lining of his gloves.
The shrink with caliper in both hands
    hunched his shoulders up
to place the two electrodes at right
    temple and right parietal arch.
He said, "OK." The anesthesiologist
    rechecked the settings on the panel
labeled Hittman, pressed the button,
    and said, "Here she goes."
The Hittman hummed its low note, and the shrink
    removed the caliper.
Her husband stood far off, feet frozen
    in two-hundred-dollar shoes.

Her Parents Brought Suit, But Since She Was Incoherent and Profane

He gazed into the uprush of the steam
    among the crystal twigs
remembering at college when they showered
    after midnight in her dorm
how fierce she turned! How her improvisations
    tested him and pleased him.
Dress-up games. Disguises. Flagrancies
    in public parks. In airplanes.
Fingertips and whispers. Teases. Thrills
    of a forbidden life.
Bohemian was how he wanted her, and made
    himself as unremarkable
as men need be: the MBA, the classic width
    of his lapel, the Tudor house,
with weekends at the club arriving
    in a fashionable choice of car
to talk collegial, congeneric talk.
    Her paintings pulled him back,
meanwhile, into a smear of orchids
    and odd persons. It was her soul.

The nurse was scanning for the signs
    of seizure: fingers, toes, a twitch,
a few goosebumps, but nothing, she said,
    "Nothing." "Right," the shrink said.
So the meterman cranked up the juice and hit it.
    Waited. Her tenth treatment.
Her resistance up. He set the knobs again,
    said, "Third time charm." Again
he boosted her. The shrink's mouth formed
    a small hurt smile. He saw
her limbs gone stiff under the storm of brainwaves
    jump, jump, jump.

And it was good—that this week she could sleep
         again; she had forgotten
their last talk, but she knew who he was,
         forgot his name, but she no longer
feared him, since the phone company did not
         control the hospital; her husband
loved her, he was not a cyborg; voices spoke,
         but she knew they did not

exist, she told herself that, and they faded.
         Now, though, the nurse's face
was in her face, the mouth was moving,
         and a voice said, "Mrs. Lindstrom,
you're awake. The treatment's over now.
         That's it. We're all done."
So there she was, this person bursting
         into tears, hearing her own voice
whimper, "No. I'm sorry. I just . . .
         Please. I'm sorry. It's OK."

IN MEMORY OF AN OLD MAPLE ON THE GROUNDS OF THE ASYLUM, BECAUSE ISAAC WEPT IN ANGER WHEN THEY FELLED IT

Dawn air moved among the youngish maple leaves. One branch thick as my little finger tip and longer than my forearm lifted a little, billowed in the mist of rain.

CYCLIST

Fog on the downhill beaded onto his forehead.
The brakepads slipped on the rims before they caught.
And the thrill of fear melted into a sudden sadness.
He walked the bike a few yards off the road, and left it
leaning on the stone fence over a birch woods,
twigs and leaves suspended in the fog
as if time had intensified.
Down where he could not see, the river
thrashed on the boulders. He had come here
twenty years ago with his sixth grade friends,
and felled a birch, and crossed on the trunk
to the island where all three of them
were kings . . . if only his feelings
could have been nostalgia for that day.
The fine fog thickened, falling,
almost rain, and he was drenched.
He shivered. It was a warm June evening,
but there was a tremor in his jaw.
A car passed unseen on the road above him
while the river passed below, and the sadness
hurt. He wanted it to be self-pity,
which he could dismiss. A sadness, though,
was almost nothing, less than the fog was
here at the birch woods' edge over the river
by the roadside. It was a broth of molecules,
a mood that comes and goes, or comes and stays.

CENTURY FLOWER

Hayden, your *Collected Shorter Poems*
reminded me just now of a century flower
on a Leeward coral ridge.

Along the path under the woody
branching-over cactus limbs and thorntrees
hermit crabs in their unwieldy shells,
their bodies grown lopsided to fit the sleeve,
trundled over the chalkdust, looking
the way I feel in this whorled English
I picked up somewhere, with sphery eyes
on chitin stalks, ridiculous sea creatures
on the mountainside among the cactuses.

Isaac, who was six then, liked
their vigilance. When they detected us,
shapes swimming in the light, vibrations
in the path, however they could tell
the predators had come, they snapped back
into their conches in a blink.

By now we were sweating under a midday sun
and straining up the mountainside, with Francie
sore a little in the knees and feet, and me
all scratched up from the bright idea I had
to see how things might look away from the path.

Here on the steep grade, when the crabs
snapped back into their shells,
without their legs to brace them,
they would teeter, and the ones that tipped

went barreling downhill past us
into the rocks and underbrush,
two, sometimes three or more at once.

Isaac laughed at them.
He looked me in the eye, and laughed.

Hayden, next to yours, my melancholy
seems almost a balm. How this may be for Isaac
I don't know. But here was a question
in his look, tender, unexpectedly, and sharp,
deliberate as the laugh was effortless
which made me laugh, and started Francie
laughing at the both of us,
all three a long time laughing
at the laughter more than anything,
with sweat-stung eyes, looking from face to face,
while those poor idiotic goddamn crabs
slammed headlong into the reef.

After a while we came
out of the cactuses and thorntrees
to a clearing where the greenest hummingbird
imaginable zipped along the now near-level path,
bobbed into the subequatorial blue sky,
and dropped beyond the ridge.

Following, we found the century flower:
lemon yellow panicles in tiers
high on a single candelabra stalk.
The surge of sap thrust up six varas
(it was a thing that wanted estimation
in no less than varas, or in English, wands).
The sap surged out of the dying fountain-shape
of fleshy broad spiked blades below

into the waxen oily yellow blooms,
hundreds of florets suffused with pulque,
pure mescal distilling into the blue.
The hummingbird drank there, the flying insects,
and the columning red ants.

    It was not metaphorical.
The century flower stood
on the promontory. You reminded me of it,
Hayden, in your book, the flower poems,
the passion for your local woods
and farms, and everywhere,
even between the dead lake and the Kmart,
sad though they may be,
festivities for the human flower too.

PRAYER BY WATER

Saturday between Good Friday
and the morning of the corpse
found missing disappeared
all day on crocuses the rain

During the feast I drank four cups of wine
and held back tears to hear my boy at seven
sing the *Ma Nishtana* to remember

Boy who led us out of Egypt Moses
boy found on the water followed
walking through the midst of water
who in anger smote the rock
to fetch us in the desert water

Old who climbing Pisgah looking down on Gilead
past Judah into the great sea died all Canaan
swimming in the heat in sight of which God
smote him and his words fell as a small rain

Whom therefore the children thirsting wept
and buried in a low place sanctified by no name

Yet remember
with a stone dropped by the doubting
here in the forgetful water

RAY

I failed, and after I had failed I saw
my failure failed to make what we call sense.
My person, meanwhile, claimed upkeep, and care,
a room, food, drink, a tad of the ancient virtue
(manhood, that would be, in Latin). I needed
mana (in Maori, soul), and manito
(in Ojibwa, god), but manhood (Sanskrit, manu)
indicated a person, preferably male.
Nouns are a covert form of the question
behind all questions, namely, *Hunh?* I'd say,
the manatee could be my manitou,
the manta ray, the leopard eagle ray,
all radiant beings in the sea, in air,
and earthbound, and in airless space dead bits
of the exploded mash from inside stars.
Who am I whom I could be here to fail?

A SHELL

The shell
my heart-muscle
extrudes
under my ribcage
is like coral.

I had thought
it was a pearl,
a smoothness
made
to soothe
my irritation.

Not so.
Edges grow
to razor-blade-
like sheerness.

Small excrescences
jut
into the flesh
which tiny shifts
abrade
and great efforts
lacerate.

It hurts
to say this.
I am afraid.

KEEPSAKE

There's no taste.
A dried rose petal,
years old,
to the tongue
inside the mouth,
feels brittle,
then soaks
pliable
though rough,
then soothing
as a roof-
of-the-mouth
blister flap
flapped into place.
Now, pasted
on ring-fingertip,
with fingerprint
clear through,
rose red gone
purple
and corrupt
with dried pus brown,
it has again
to a shy thumb
that fresh
tenderness of silk
and smells,
though sourish,
like new.

ON THE INUNDATED FIRST SITE OF
THE TOWN OF GREENVILLE

Spoonbill catfish big as Confederate soldiers
rout in the mud under uninterruptable darkness.
Gaspergou make mournful drumming.

Where did the cottonwoods grow in the yards
when the wind god laid his lip to the flue,
blundering like a small-town flautist?

Somewhere broken brick lies feathered
by fine silt. Snagged loops
of a rusted cable rot
in the rootwreck of a cypress.

Years ago, just here, where the muddy river
wrinkles and comes unwrinkled,
there was a bonewhite sandbar. Friends
on a warm night lay there, keeping the dawn watch,
talking. Near midheaven, meteors streamed
out of the eyes of Perseus, and the boy's hand slid
to the largest knuckle under her waistband.

What did the river do with the sandgrains
shaken out of her long hair?
Where is the sizzle her breath made
cooling her clenched teeth and her tonguetip?
What's left now of the jurisdiction of gooseflesh?

TWO LADIES

The blacktop here, the way it curves
between the rows of maples over the half-mown meadow
past the pond, is beautiful, I tell houseguests,
and people nod, which only tweaks my urge
to say what moves me, now especially, during the hour
before sunset, when the light and shadow
on the maple trunks, and on the twin birch
where the road bends, gleam with an inexplicable power.
Leaning here, you feel bark crumble
into your palm, smell mown grass in the exhaust,
hawk, spit, step one step sideways,
and the cosmos comes in from another angle.
It's too much! Light
delves into a clump of white snakeroot,
and the Beauty blazing into thought
feels, somehow, indeterminate,
although the mower blade says,
always, and precisely, "This!"
Five hundred years ago, I saw two ladies
standing in the prow of a unmanned wherry. The soul
in armor stepped aboard. "Good journey to you all!"
I said, and Beauty gazed into the bottom of the lake,
hands folded together on Her low, round stomach.
The darker Lady looked at the armored soul
as if She were about to smile,
and the boat steered toward the invisible island.

JIG FOR THE INSANE ASYLUM
GATEHOUSE NOW CONDEMNED

My fingers slap the tone holes,
skip, and twiddle, tonguetip
strikes the breath, eyes
staggering ahead
and down the page—the pitch,
the rhythm, unperformable
in verse. Behind my eardrum
hair cells, of all organs
keenest to the sleights of time,
in warm air, vibrate, in a bony
snailshell in the skull,
minutely differentiating. Soon
bulldozers will come
and cross the room where now Bach
breathes into a two-bit whistle
and dead peasants dance.

GIOTTO'S ANGEL OVER THE DEAD CHRIST
SPREAD HIS ARMS IN FLIGHT

Blue violets are back beside the road,
each upper pair of petals splayed
as if in pain to let a wound go deeper.
In the cream cleft purple veins trail off.
The lower petals meet with white
pubescences on either side,
and under that a fifth, more fluted petal
forms the channel inward from below.

Inside, orange tips of carpels form
a pyramid sprung through
by the stigmata, milkwhite, moist, I know,
because I picked, and pulled apart,
and left a flower with the crooked stem gone limp,
used tissue dropped into the deepening grass.

And you, just now, I made you laugh.
I took your hand. You wept.
I nailed your body into a flimsy box.

Here, the flower ancient poets set
in songs for courtesans to sing them back,
the Chinese plum, opens out of a jagged branch.
I wanted to say, again. But as we know,
the one time opening, it tears.
A petal falls. Ten thousand petals
trip into the gust along a certain street.

Giotto's Angel Over the Dead Christ Spread His Arms in Flight

Again, I wanted to say, under the plum bark
an old stirring pushes the blossom
out of another branch.
And you, I feel your fingers
working open even the softest part.

FURTHER REVELATIONS ON THE
PLANET WOKKA

While I stood holding the car door for him,
He said, "Thirty ultra-scorpions a day"—
That's how much he ate on his home planet—
Scorpions the size of housecats. He kept
Talking, but in my ear the voice trailed off
While I looked down at the smartweed blooming
Beside the hot asphalt with little spikes
Of three-seamed footballs in pink satin slips.
Later, I found out underneath the pink
The seeds are black and lustrous, though I found some
Nut-brown, some a translucent milk of amber,
And I read that smartweed is a kind of buckwheat
Growing, the field guide puts it, in "waste places."
Isaac talked nonstop while I looked down
At the way the pink heads of the smartweed
Stood with the jointed stems bending a little
And the blades of leaf lolled into a rich light,
Mind turned inside out in bloom among them,
Rooting into the salt dust by the road,
When Isaac shouted, "Dad! This is my sword!"
He showed me the imaginary blade,
Looking me in the face hard. "So, you want one?"
After my palm sprung closed on what he gave me,
I shook the grip to feel the tang inside it,
Nodded, and he nodded back. The two of us
Then stood as swordsmen on the planet Wokka.

ONE MORE THING

1. *Auschwitz*

Pikkolo Jean picked Primo Levi from the work detail
to cross the Lager one fair June day
and fetch soup. The way back, lugging
broth of cabbages and turnips
on a wooden pole between them, would be hard—
before that, though, it was an easy hour's walk,
and Jean, who spoke good French and German,
wondered if his friend would take this time
to give a lesson in Italian. Levi,
not quite knowing why, began to speak,
and translate bit by bit, the canto
where among the evil counsellors in Hell
Dante and Virgil met two men on fire.
"The greater of the ancient horns of flame then
trembled, murmuring, as in a wind . . ."
It was Ulysses, with his quick mind
still intact, and from inside the fire he told
how he had asked his men to sail beyond
the Gates of Hercules into the lower world.

2. *Athens*

Ammianus Marcellinus said
that Socrates in prison
waiting for the hemlock
heard this poem Stesichorus had made
two hundred years before:

> Forget the wars, and sing.
> This Phrygian flute
> remembers phrasework
> of the very Graces,
> and the swallows
> jabber, and say nothing
> but that it is spring.

The young musician sang
so skillfully that Socrates
implored him, could he teach
an old man such a lyric
in the time they had?

And when the rhapsode
asked him why, the old man
said: "I want to die
knowing one more thing."

THE LAST CONFESSION
OF ROGER TORY PETERSON

To see the yellow-bellied sapsucker suck sap,
to watch the oystercatcher at his catch,
and bluebird, woodcock, dickcissel, blue goose,
in bush to find them worth more than in hand . . .
to my mind just to list their names does much
as the tufted titmouse cock's cry does the hen:
Peter peter peter! *Here here here*!
If ever a purple gallinule highstepped
and clucked across a trembling lily pad,
if ever an *anser* answered from the fog,
let buteos be buteos, let whimbrels have
their whim, may limpkins be my lambkins now,
and my works work to call the killdeer dear.

LIRIODENDRON TULIPIFERA

When I considered the tulip tree,
for the orange, cream,
and pale green cup of blossom,

when I thought about the butteriness of the wood
peeled over the gliding tongue of a plane,
the moldings easily worked by knife,

when I considered the shade
where tulips drop by the hundred in late March,
fresh-looking still, as though they fell too soon,

when I pronounced the names—
magnolia, whitewood,
white and yellow poplar,

when I could stand in clear sight of the boles,
straight, taller even than an oak,
when I could pay true mind,

I walked among them, it was late,
and the wind came trembling
into the dusk among the leaves.

IN A DROWSE BY THE AUTUMNAL WATERS

Hands on the steering wheel strummed almost leaden
by the hot treads pressing the asphalt,
by the sleep of the crankshaft in the crankcase,
I was soaring, half awake,
late monarchs, with the flame on each wing
caught in a black craze, gust-borne
over the asters at the woods' edge,
over the ragweed, and along the river.

ONE FALL

Leaves dropped all day
onto the shallow creek
and slipped away,
clear water folded
with clear shadows
getting deep,
until the brown leaves
rolled down
where not even the lightning
showed them while they sank.

AGAIN CONSIDER THE WIND

The wind continuing to turn and turn back
in its turning does not sing,
though in December it may strike
the living maple twigs with crystal and chrome hammers,
and the chords, which are not music, wake the soul.
A man pries loose a frozen wedge of clay
from the lip of a posthole for a barbed wire fence.
His life is half past, and his arm feels strong.
He throws, and the icepane vibrates
under the tongue-shaped clod sent strumming
out to the midpoint of the pond.
Again the wind tears into a prolonged howl
between the frozen, rotten planks of the little dock.
The sun is small and low, and lower.
What has turned will turn back in its turning
and the sound where tiny spurs of ice rake
through the splintered grain of slash pine
over the dock (which this spring someone must repair),
the rasping noise he hears, is not a whisper.
Solstice at this moment ends the year.
The young pines on the ridge south of the pond
bend northward so that the tops all waveringly
indicate Polaris, which is always there.
Reading prophetic discourse into the wind
is fool's work, and the fool's
great uncle's best friend from his childhood
drove this nail through this plank into the crossbeam
with three strokes so that the steel rang, I was there,
and the wind carried the music across the pond.

A NOTE ABOUT THE AUTHOR

Brooks Haxton, born in Greenville, Mississippi, in 1950, has published two book-length narrative poems, *Dead Reckoning* and *The Lay of Eleanor and Irene*, and two collections of poems, *Dominion* and *Traveling Company*. He teaches at Syracuse University and at the Warren Wilson College MFA Program for Writers. He is also the scriptwriter for an American Masters Series Film, *Tennessee Williams: Orpheus of the American Stage*. Recipient of many honors including fellowships from the National Endowment for the Arts, the New York Foundation for the Arts, and the Ingram Merrill Foundation, he lives in Syracuse with his wife and children.

A NOTE ON THE TYPE

The text of this book is set in Linotype Garamond No. 3. It is not a true copy of any of the designs of Claude Garamond (1480–1561), but an adaptation of his types, which set the European standard for two centuries. It probably owes as much to the designs of Jean Jannon, a Protestant printer working in Sedan in the early seventeenth century, who had worked with Garamond's romans earlier, in Paris, and who was denied their use because of the Catholic censorship. Jannon's matrices came into the possession of the Imprimerie Nationale, where they were thought to be by Garamond himself, and so described when the Imprimerie revived the type in 1900. This particular version is based on an adaptation by Morris Fuller Benton.

Composition by Heritage Printers
Charlotte, North Carolina
Printed and bound by Quebecor Printing,
Kingsport, Tennessee
Designed by Harry Ford